THE FLANNEL MAKERS
A brief history of the Welsh Woollen Industry

Welsh Crafts Series:

1. THE FLANNEL MAKERS
A Brief History of the Welsh Woollen Industry
J. Geraint Jenkins

**2. DRE-FACH FELINDRE
AND THE WOOLLEN INDUSTRY**
J. Geraint Jenkins

WELSH CRAFTS

The Flannel Makers

A brief history of the Welsh Woollen Industry

J. Geraint Jenkins

Gwasg Carreg Gwalch

Published by Gwasg Carreg Gwalch in 2005.

ISBN: 0-86381-963-X

Gwasg Carreg Gwalch,
12 Iard yr Orsaf, Llanrwst, Conwy, Cymru (Wales)
LL26 0EH
Tel: 01492 642031   Fax: 01492 641502
e-mail: books@carreg-gwalch.co.uk website: www.carreg-gwalch.co.uk
Printed and published in Wales.

Acknowledgements

Illustrations are by David Coviello, the National Museum and Galleries of Wales,
Museum of Welsh Life, Trefriw Woollen Mill, Cambrian Mill, Melin Tregwynt,
Arthur Thomas (Ffatri Penmachno), Newtown Textile Museum, Curlew Weavers
and Gwasg Carreg Gwalch.

A Glossary of Welsh place-names

Bro Morgannwg	*Vale of Glamorgan*
Brynbuga	*Usk*
Caerdydd	*Cardiff*
Caerfyrddin	*Carmarthen*
Casnewydd	*Newport* (Gwent)
Dinbych-y-pysgod	*Tenby*
Hwlffordd	*Haverfordwest*
Maldwyn	*Montgomeryshire*
Morgannwg	*Glamorgan*
Penrhyn Gŵyr	*Gower*
Sir Ddinbych	*Denbighshire*
Sir Gaerfyrddin	*Carmarthenshire*
Sir Faesyfed	*Radnorshire*
Y Drenewydd	*Newtown*
Ynys Môn	*Anglesey*

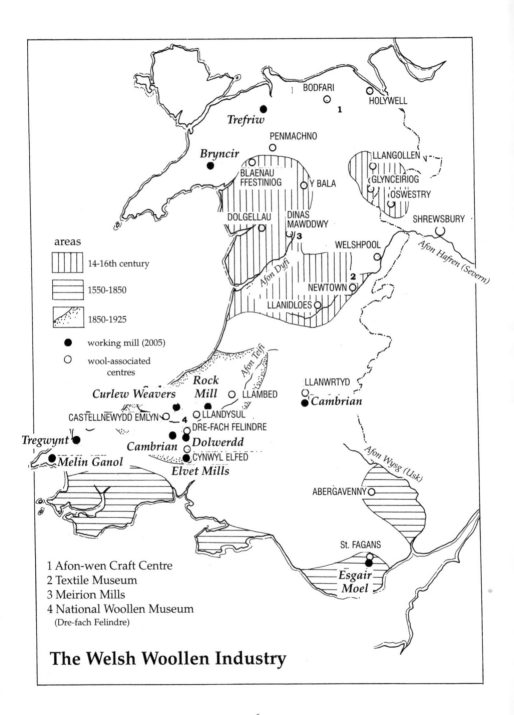

The Welsh Woollen Industry

BODFARI
HOLYWELL
1
Trefriw
PENMACHNO
Bryncir
LLANGOLLEN
BLAENAU
FFESTINIOG
Y BALA
GLYNCEIRIOG
OSWESTRY
DOLGELLAU
DINAS
MAWDDWY
SHREWSBURY
3
WELSHPOOL
Afon Hafren (Severn)
areas

14-16th century

1550-1850

1850-1925

● working mill (2005)

○ wool-associated
centres

2
NEWTOWN
LLANIDLOES

Afon Dyfi

Afon Teifi
Rock
Mill
LLAMBED
LLANWRTYD
Curlew Weavers
Cambrian
CASTELLNEWYDD EMLYN
4
LLANDYSUL
DRE-FACH FELINDRE
Tregwynt
Cambrian
Dolwerdd
CYNWYL ELFED
Melin Ganol
Elvet Mills

Afon Wysg (Usk)

ABERGAVENNY

St. FAGANS

1 Afon-wen Craft Centre
2 Textile Museum
3 Meirion Mills
4 National Woollen Museum
  (Dre-fach Felindre)

Esgair
Moel

The Welsh Woollen Industry

Introduction

From the Middle Ages until the mid-nineteenth century, woollen manufacturing was among the most important of Welsh industries. It was certainly the most widespread, for it was impossible to move any distance without meeting some evidence for the existence of this important industry. The textile worker, whether he worked in the home or in a factory building was as essential to the rural community as the blacksmith or carpenter, for there was hardly a parish in the land that did not have its contingent of spinners and weavers, dyers and fullers.

In some parts of the country the manufacture of woollen goods went beyond the stage of supplying a self-sufficing rural community with its day-to-day essentials, for in those districts, manufacturers were concerned with producing flannel and cloth that was exported to all parts of the world. In the heyday of the industry Welsh cloth clothed the slaves of North America as well as the armies of the Duke of Wellington; Welsh flannel was worn by coalminers and steel workers; it was deemed to possess 'a peculiar softness of texture which renders them exceedingly well adapted to be worn next to the skin of the most delicate invalid' and fortunes were made by those concerned with its manufacture. The old county of Trefaldwyn in particular, possessed all the natural advantages of raw materials and water supply that could have made it into a textile manufacturing district as important as the West Riding of Yorkshire. Newtown, the centre of the industry, was known to early nineteenth century travellers as 'the Leeds of Wales'; indeed it was truly a 'new town' built round the nucleus of the ancient borough of Llanfair-yng-Nghedewain.

The history of the Welsh woollen industry may be divided into four periods:
1.   From the early fourteenth century to the mid-sixteenth century when textile production was developed as a domestic industry in southern Wales, particularly in the south-west (Sir Benfro - *Pembrokeshire*) and Gwent.
2.   From about 1546 to the mid-nineteenth century when the counties of northern Wales; Maldwyn (*Montgomeryshire*),

Carding and spinning at Betws-y-coed, Conwy.
A tourist photograph of Elen Lloyd

Meirionnydd and the south of Sir Ddinbych (*Denbighshire*) reigned supreme as centres of the industry.

3.   From about 1850 to 1920 when the industry was concentrated in western Wales, especially in the Teifi valley.

Of course throughout the centuries there were textile workers outside the main regions of concentration. Until the end of the nineteenth century, small comprehensive mills were vital to the economy of every rural society. The Esgair Moel Woollen Mill, preserved at the Museum of Welsh Life, was of this type. From its establishment in the mid-eighteenth century it was concerned entirely with supplying a local market and it never entered the highly competitive trade channelled through such centres as Bristol, Shrewsbury and London. Its customers were local farmers who brought fleeces to the mill. This was spun into yarn and woven into cloth or blankets for the farmer's family.

The domestic craft
Until the beginning of the fourteenth century, woollen manufacturing was a domestic craft practised throughout Wales. The inhabitants of the country obtained wool from their own flocks and with simple equipment they produced the knitting yarn and blankets, cloth and flannel that they themselves required. Wool was carded with teasels or thistles that grew everywhere: it was spun with a simple spindle and whorl and woven into cloth on a warp-weighted loom. The Welsh were a people, said Giraldus Cambrensis in the twelfth century, 'with a wide experience of woollen manufacturing but who paid no attention to industry or commerce'. The coarse cloth or brychan that was manufactured in all parts of Wales contributed to the self-sufficiency of medieval rural communities but it made no contribution at all to the export trade.

In the Middle Ages, the surplus of raw wool obtained from the small scraggy sheep of the time, that was not required to meet local needs, was exported. Much of this was sent to Flanders, the main textile producing region of Europe at the time. A levy had to be charged on all exported wool and, in order to make the collection of the levy a much easier matter, it was decreed that all

A fulling mill at Pontarddulais. The fulling mill revolutionised the woollen industry and marked its first stage in transfer from cottage to mill building.

Skeins of wool drying at Ffatri Penmachno, northern Wales.

wool had to be exported through selected towns, known as 'staple towns'. In 1327 Caerdydd (*Cardiff*), Caerfyrddin (*Carmarthen*), Hwlffordd (*Haverfordwest*) and Shrewsbury were designated staple towns, but within twenty years the sole staple for Wales was Carmarthen. It was soon realised by the merchants that Carmarthen was not the ideal centre for export of Welsh wool to Flanders and the woolmen were allowed to take their wool to any English staple town that they wished. Many even took wool on teams of pack-horses on the long overland journey to King's Lynn. By the beginning of the fifteenth century, the amount of wool exported from Wales had declined very greatly, for a large proportion of the wool produced in the country was being absorbed by the growing cloth manufacturing industry within its own borders.

The genesis of an industry

By the middle of the fourteenth century, great changes were taking place in Wales. Less raw wool was being exported and large quantities of cloth were being exported through southern Wales seaports to Bristol. From Bristol, they were re-exported to many parts of the European continent: to Gascony, Brittany, France, Portugal and Iceland. Cloth was taken by sea from such ports as Tenby, Haverfordwest and Carmarthen but it was also sold at fairs such as those held in the Gwent towns of Y Fenni (*Abergavenny*), Brynbuga (*Usk*), Casnewydd (*Newport*) and Caerleon. The markets of the English borderlands – Ludlow, Shrewsbury and Hereford were also visited frequently by Welsh cloth merchants in the fifteenth century. Some clothiers, especially from Gwent, conveyed their goods on horseback to the great annual cloth fair of Saint Bartholomew in London. All in all, the fourteenth century was a century of change in the woollen trade for cloth manufacturing ceased to be merely a domestic craft contributing to the needs of the local population only, for it emerged as a true commercial venture; an industry rather than a domestic pursuit.

By the mid-fifteenth century, Shrewsbury, a town that was to play a vital role in the development of the Welsh textile industry in succeeding centuries was already attaining a position of eminence

The Great Wheel that replaced the primitive spindle and whorl.

in the sale of Welsh cloth. The town authorities were so worried 'that in order to protect their own industrial population, forbade the buying or bringing into town of any Welsh cloth'. But their protests and anger were to no avail, for the weavers of Wales became more and more dependent on the Shrewsbury market for the sale of their cloths. The main centres of cloth manufacture in the fourteenth century were the counties of southern Wales – Penfro (*Pembrokeshire*), Sir Gaerfyrddin (*Carmarthenshire*), Bro Morgannwg (*Vale of Glamorgan*), Penrhyn Gŵyr (*Gower*) and Gwent. It was still a domestic industry for wool was still carded, spun and woven in the cottages and farmhouses of Wales, but now production was for the international market rather than for a local one.

One of the main reasons for the change of emphasis was a technical one, for new devices, new techniques and new equipment replaced those that had probably been in use since prehistoric times:
1.   The spindle and whorl was replaced by the wheel for spinning.
2.   The horizontal loom with healds, beams, shuttle and pedals replaced the warp-weighted loom.
3.   Cloth could be finished and thickened under the hammers of a water-driven fulling mill. The adoption of the fulling mill and its dependence on water power, marked the first stage in the transference of the woollen industry from cottage to factory.

The Pandy
The place-name *Pandy* or *Melin Ban* indicates the location of fulling mills. Until the very end of the eighteenth century, carding, spinning and weaving were carried out in the homes of the people using hand-operated equipment. But from the fourteenth century onwards, cloth had to be shrunk and thickened under the hammers of water-driven fulling mills. Fuller's earth, human urine and soda were applied to the cloth. The original method of fulling was to place cloth in a stream and allow men to walk on it for hours; indeed, even in the eighteenth century fulling mills were still described as 'Walk Mills'.

Although Pembrokeshire had more fulling mills than any other county in the fourteenth century, they were also well known in Carmarthenshire, Morgannwg (*Glamorgan*), Gwent and even in Sir Ddinbych. It has often been said that the growth of the Welsh woollen industry in general and the introduction of fulling mills in particular was the result of the settlement of Flemish weavers in Pembrokeshire. Undoubtedly the important and widespread

Wallis Mill, Ambleston, Pembrokeshire. A Pandy *(fulling mill) was located at Ambleston in the 15th century and it could well have been at Wallis.*

changes attributed to the Flemings have been greatly exaggerated for the first wave of immigrants in the twelfth century came too early and the second wave in the 1330s too late to explain the establishment of fulling mills in Wales. Between 1300 and 1330 at least 71 pandai were built in Wales.

In addition to the technical innovations of the fourteenth century, there were other reasons for the prosperity of Welsh textile manufacturing. During the course of the century, the woollen industry of Flanders which had taken so much Welsh raw wool was declining and it could no longer supply Britain with finished cloth as in past centuries. The government of the day encouraged the woollen industry in England and Wales by levying a high duty on exports of raw wool but a low duty on exports of finished cloth.

The decline of the industry in south-western Wales

Although in general, textile manufacturing in Wales was not organized, there were Guilds of Fullers and Weavers in

Fulling equipment at Penmachno, 1968.

Carmarthen; a town that was especially important as a centre of trade and manufacture in the late Middle Ages. Members of the guilds guarded their rights very jealously and they attempted to prevent the development of the industry outside the town, in the cottages and farmhouses of the surrounding countryside. The restrictive practices of the guilds discouraged all textile manufacturers who became far readier to set up their workshops in the freer atmosphere of northern Wales far away from the dampening influence of the guilds. By 1600, the export of cloth from Pembrokeshire had virtually ceased and George Owen of Henllys, the county's historian, laments 'The trade of clothing used in tymes past in this countrie ys now utterly neglected'. Wool from Pembrokeshire was sold in Cardigan market to 'woolmen from northern Wales and by them woven into white cloth which they again sold to men from Shrewsbury'.

According to tradition, woollen manufacturing declined in south-western Wales due to an epidemic of 'sweating sickness', but a more likely explanation lay in the fact that coal, not cloth became

Hand carding using metal cards

A water-driven carding engine that gradually replaced hand cards in late 18th century Powys.

the chief item of export. Cloth was still sold in local markets and fairs, but to a great extent textile manufacturing in southern Wales reverted to being a local industry contributing to the economic self-sufficiency of the rural neighbourhood.

Tenter frame for drying cloth at Ffatri Penmachno with the mill owner, John Rees Jones, and one of his employees, Richie Thomas, the well-known tenor.

Wool scales at Ffatri Penmachno.

Penmachno workers in 1928. The mill was registered as 'Hannah Jones & Son'.

The industry in northern and central Wales 1560-1790

The scattered industry

'I thincke and judge that God and Nature hathe appointed the inhabitants of those partes to lyve by cloathinge onely.'

In the calmer conditions following the Act of Union and well away from the restrictive influence of the guilds, the woollen industry in northern and central Wales developed very rapidly in the sixteenth century. Again the progress of the industry was marked by the establishment of numerous *pandai* (fulling mills) along the banks of the swiftly flowing streams. Indeed so many fulling mills were set up between 1540 and 1700 that the industry never became located in a few river valleys as in Yorkshire. The plentiful supply of swiftly running water proved almost an embarrassment, for the woollen industry became so widespread that it could never develop as a fully integrated, concentrated industrial complex within a limited region. Industrial development, for what it was, developed in numerous narrow valleys and it depended for its raw material on the fleeces of small, scraggy sheep that grazed unhindered on the bleak mountains, moors and upland plateaus.

Fulling was the only process carried out in a mill building, for carding and spinning were carried out by women in their own homes, using hand cards and 'a great wheel'. Weaving demanded more expensive equipment than that required for the preparation of yarn, so that weaving became the responsibility of more prosperous people who could afford to buy hand-looms. Most of the weaving masters were farmers and until the mid-eighteenth century, farm labourers were hired at fairs at such places as Machynlleth and Llanidloes to work at the looms as well as in the fields. On many farms, one or two looms would be kept in an out-house or lean-to shed that was known as a tŷ gwŷdd (loom house) for use when farm work slackened off in winter.

The location of the industry

The woollen industry between 1560 and 1790, although widely distributed throughout northern and central Wales, was really concentrated in three distinct regions. The other districts of Gwynedd and Powys, in addition to supplying local demand, were mainly concerned with supplying spun yarn to the manufacturers of those three regions. The regions were:

1. MONTGOMERYSHIRE especially the Severn valley where flannel was produced.
2. MEIRIONNYDD where coarse white cloth called 'strong cloth' or 'high country cloth' was the main product. The isolated homesteads around Dolgellau and Dinas Mawddwy were important producers of cloth.
3. DENBIGHSHIRE especially the Ceiriog valley and the area around Llangollen. The local, very coarse white cloth produced was known as 'small cloth'.

Products of the industry

Flannel A plain woven, fairly thin cloth that was usually undyed. The word was used as early as 1503 and Wales was regarded as the special seat of flannel manufacture. A piece of Montgomeryshire flannel was from 100 to 132 yards long and 7/8 of a yard wide.

Strong Cloth or High Country Cloth A coarse, thick white cloth. A piece of strong cloth produced in Meirionnydd was known as 'a web' and each web was 200 yards long and 7/8 of a yard wide.

Small Cloth A very rough cloth abounding with long white hairs ('kemp'). In the Ceiriog valley a piece of small cloth was 200 yards long and $^3/_4$ of a yard wide.

Linsey A strong white cloth made from a mixture of flax and wool. Flax was at one time widely grown in the Severn valley. The place name of a village Arddleen (*Gardd* [garden] and *llin* [flax]) suggests the importance of flax growing in Montgomeryshire .

Crimsi Rough cloth usually consisting of red stripes on a grey background.

Cottons This was not made of cotton, but it refers to the art of cottoning. This was the process of raising the nap of rough cloth with teasels to give a soft fluffy appearance.

Wadmoll Rough undressed cloth used by saddlers for covering horse collars and saddles.

Weighing and Measuring Cloth in the seventeenth and eighteenth centuries

Wool was weighed by the sack. A sack was 364 pounds.

A Tod of Wool	=	28 pounds
13 Tods	=	1 sack
1 Tod	=	4 nails
1 Nail	=	7 pounds

Linear measurement was by the yard which varied from 35 inches to 37 inches. Another important measurement was the ell.

1 ell = $44\frac{7}{8}$ inches – 45 inches

A goade was 55 inches

A length of flannel was known as a 'frieze' and this was between 100 yards and 132 yards in length.

The Shrewsbury drapers

In the sixteenth century Welsh weavers had to sell all their products to the Shrewsbury Drapers' Company, a medieval craft guild, who took the cloth to the Cloth Market at Blackwell Hall in London for export to all parts of the world.

In the sixteenth century the main market was the town of Oswestry and there every Monday, weavers from central and northern Wales met the Shrewsbury Drapers to sell their products. There was no market hall and the weavers met the Drapers in houses. In addition to the weekly Monday market, there were also three big fairs in May, August and November. Cloth was brought to Oswestry by pack horses, but many of the weavers were very poor and could not afford horses and 'not havinge other cariage by reason of their povertie doe use to carry theyr friezes on theyr backes and heades to Oswestrie market'. Very soon the Shrewsbury Drapers' Company became dissatisfied with arrangements at Oswestry. There was no proper market and the eighteen mile journey from Shrewsbury to Oswestry was a difficult one because it was a road infested with highwaymen. In 1621 they resolved that they would not go again to Oswestry to buy Welsh cloth and the Market Hall at Shrewsbury became the only place where Welsh cloth was sold. The Shrewsbury Market survived until about 1775.

Ffatri Penmachno – power loom

The industry in north and mid-Wales 1790-1840

Mechanisation and the growth of towns

Changes in marketing

Until the last quarter of the eighteenth century, the Shrewsbury Drapers' Company bought almost all the cloth of Wales and members of the Company obtained great wealth as a result of trade with the weavers of northern and central Wales. By 1788 they were losing their power because:

1.   Wales was opened up by the roads and much more flannel was being produced.

2.   Buyers from other towns, especially Liverpool began sending agents to Wales to buy Welsh cloth. No longer was it necessary for Welsh weavers to make the long journey to Shrewsbury to meet their buyers.

'Until these few years the only market was held weekly on Thursdays at Shrewsbury, when they were exposed to sale in a hall belonging to the drapers of that town and where no buyer but of that particular fraternity was admitted. But lately the manufacturers have had the good fortune of the market in their own houses and the drapers the well deserved pleasure of employing buyers by commission . . . who frequently purchased pieces before they were out of the loom. Ever since . . . the face of the country has changed much for the better and the baneful effects of imposition and disappointment begin to disappear.'

In 1832 a Market Hall (now the Regent Leisure Centre) was built in Newtown and in 1836 the Market Hall at Llanidloes was built.

Mechanisation

Until about 1790, the woollen industry in central and northern Wales was a mere supplement to farming, but after that date it developed into a true industry, especially in Montgomeryshire. Until then, the land produced all the wool required; it was carded, spun and woven in the home and the small proportion that was

The water-driven spinning mule that replaced the spinning wheel in early 19th century Powys.

dyed could be dyed with vegetable colouring agents in the home. A fulling mill was to be found within walking distance of a weaving shop, and with the establishment of a flannel exchange, the flannel could be sold within the region itself.

The most significant development of the late eighteenth century, however, was mechanisation of some of the textile processes. The first piece of machinery to be adopted was the carding engine, which replaced the traditional hand cards. These were water-driven machines and as a result of their widespread adoption after 1790 the domestic hand carding of wool was a thing of the past. The first carding factory in northern Wales was set up in 1794 at Dolobran, near Meifod, Montgomeryshire , where carding engines were installed in an old iron forge run by the Lloyd family, a family famed for being the founders of Lloyd's Bank. In both Meirionnydd and Sir Drefaldwyn water power from an already existing corn or fulling mill was often adapted for carding, so that many a northern Wales pandy developed into a textile factory where the first and last processes of cloth manufacture were concentrated.

A weaving shop at Newtown, Powys. Weaving shops that accommodated hand-looms were found on the upper floors of cottage dwellings.

For a while the domestic spinners struggled on, but their days were numbered for by 1815 the spinning jenny was becoming well-known amongst the textile workers of northern Wales. Although the jenny was at first a hand-operated machine, its size was such that it had to be accommodated in a special building and it would never fit into a cottage kitchen. More often than not the jenny joined the fulling stocks and carding engine in a factory building and with the adoption of water-driven improvements to the jenny, power from a stream to operate the spinning equipment became vital.

By 1820 a typical Montgomeryshire woollen mill was a riverside building with water-driven carders, spinning mules or jacks and fulling stocks within it. Textile manufacturing became a valley

A Newtown 'truck shop' associated with all weaving establishments.

occupation, never to return to the isolated cottages and farmhouses of upland Wales.

While carding and spinning had joined fulling and dyeing as factory processes before 1820, the highly skilled process of weaving did not become part of this complex until well into the nineteenth century. Until the 1850s, power looms were not successful, for as the contemporary writer said 'the power loom does not work without the tenderness of a skilful human hand'. It was a great advantage, however, for the hand-loom weaver to locate his shop as near as possible to the source of raw material – the carding and spinning factory. Gradually a factory system entered the weaving industry, especially in Montgomeryshire and although a certain amount of weaving was still practised in remote farmhouses, the towns and villages, especially Llanidloes and Newtown became the all-important centres of the weaving industry. The tall, three or four-floored buildings with their numerous windows bear witness to this day of the importance of wool in the history of Montgomeryshire . A weaving factory occupying perhaps the third and fourth floors of a building stretched over many cottage dwellings, usually of the 'back to back' variety. The factory was usually entered by an outside staircase at the back of the terrace. In many cases the owner of a weaving factory was also the owner of a shop at the end of the row. These shops were the notorious 'truck shops' or 'tommy shops' and on applying for work, a weaver was always asked for the number of persons in his family; the bigger the family, the better were his chances of obtaining work.

Newtown – the Leeds of Wales

Until the last decade of the eighteenth century Newtown, or Llanfair-yng-Nghedewain, was little more than a small market town, catering for the needs of an agricultural hinterland. When Robert Owen left his native town in the early seventeen-eighties it was but 'a very small market town . . . a neat beautifully situated town with the ordinary trades, but no manufactures except for a very few flannel looms'. By 1790 the inhabitants included one weaver, one card-maker, one flannel manufacturer and one woolstapler, but cloth manufacturing was no more important than it was in Llanfair Caereinion or Rhaeadr. By 1797, however, there were great changes afoot and Arthur Aikin, on his tour in 1797, found 'infant factories', although as yet they were of 'little consequence'. The Rev. J. Evans, on his tour in 1798, noted that manufacturing was 'increasing every day' while another traveller six years later described the manufactures as 'extensive in scale and "masterly" in methods'. Walter Davies, when he carried out his survey in 1799, describes how 'of late the powerful agency of water has been brought to their assistance, and about 40 carding and several spinning machines have been erected in different parts of the country . . . there are manufactories upon larger scales . . . several at Newtown'.

By the turn of the century therefore, carding, spinning, and fulling mills, as well as weaving shops, were to be found in

The Newtown Flannel Exchange

Newtown.

The outbreak of the Napoleonic wars put a temporary brake on factory building for a few years, and this even ruined the owner of the first factory, the Dingle, which was erected near the town in 1798.

Nevertheless, the slowing down of factory building was only temporary and during the first decade of the nineteenth century, yarn factories and weaving shops were established by the dozen. In this development the name of a local clergyman, the Rev. G.A. Evors, occurs frequently. Evors came to occupy Newtown Hall about 1806 'leaving his southern Wales parish in charge of a curate. He was long the only resident magistrate in Newtown, where for about forty years he was able to lord it like a petty benevolent despot'. Evors was not a manufacturer himself but he spent considerable sums of money in putting up new factories or renovating old ones, and letting them out to manufacturers at substantial rents.

Evors built houses and weaving factories and undoubtedly accumulated a huge fortune. He died in 1844 in suspicious circumstances with £8,000 on his person, after an overdose of laudanum. Another local man, William Tilsley, a Newtown banker, built the Milford carding mill in 1809 and another in the town around 1812. These he rented to manufacturers. Tilsley sought to increase the water power to his mills by building a weir across the river. This landed him in a lawsuit with Evors who claimed that he himself had 'the right of Free Warren and Fishery in the Severn for nine mills from Scafell to Gorrandu pools'.

The right of weiring was rented to Tilsley for £20 a year, but in 1831 Tilsley's bank failed and he was forced to sell his two mills to pay his creditors.

The prosperity of Newtown as a centre of flannel manufacturing was reflected in the rapid rise in population:

1771 –   c.800
1801 –   990
1811 –   2,025
1821 –   3,486
1831 –   4,550

In 1821 a branch of the Shropshire canal, which had reached Garthmyl a few years earlier, was extended to Newtown. By 1825 there was a regular service between Newtown and Manchester; the journey taking six days at a cost of 35 pence per hundredweight. The opening of the Newtown-Builth road in the same year made it possible to send flannel by cart and wagon to southern Wales.

Trade directories give some indication of the scale of production in the town, although the figures in some cases may be exaggerated. In 1823, there were fifty-four flannel manufacturers, in 1828 there were sixty-five, while in 1830 flannel manufacturers numbered eighty-one.

The amazing progress of Newtown was expressed in a poem of 1833 by Robyn Ddu Eryri:

An address to Newtown Montgomeryshire

Oh what a blissful place! By Severn's Banks so fair
Happy the Inhabitants; and wholesome is thy Air,
Nine years long, since last I've seen thee fled
Ah! when departing, my Heart in grief has bled.
Thy lasses fair and thy young men as kind
Thy flannel fine and generous every mind
But now, tis now, I wonder most
I see thy Improvements, well can thy townsmen boast
To London great, in short by the canal
Thy flannel goes, as quick as one can tell,
And thence from there, the Flannel's quickly hurled
To every part of Britain, and its known world;
The gaslight bright, thy new built houses high,
Thy factories lofts, seem smiling on the sky
Newtown, Newtown is surely now thy name
Britannia whole is joyful of thy fame;
Adieu Welsh Pool, thy Market swift is falling
Newtown's new Market Halls is daily blooming
Auspicious building, Wales' greatest grandeur
Cambria's masterpiece, Manufacturer's pleasure;
New Bank, New Church, New Halls of great renown
New houses, new Flannel new gas in brave Newtown

Go on and flourish, thy Markets ever bless
With flannel, full of Money and success.

Robert Parry or Robyn Ddu Eryri

Newtown, 3rd Oct., 1833

Life in Newtown was not as prosperous as the poet imagined, for although there were prolonged periods of prosperity, there were far too many periods of depression when discontent and unemployment were rife. 'The Weavers' is the most depressed of all trades' said Richard Evans in his evidence to the Royal Commission on Handloom Weavers in 1837. 'Children get into the loom and take the weaver's work from him at under price . . . the men are underselling one another'. Although periods of prosperity attracted as many as 300 weavers from other districts to Newtown, the frequent periods of depression meant that many left the town for the textile factories of Lancashire and Yorkshire, and even Sir Fflint, while others emigrated to America. 'The trade is subject to fluctuations', says the Handloom Weaver's Report, 'owing to the various prices of wool and from casual over-supply'.

Wages on the whole were low; in 1837 for example, they were as follows:

1	Sorting by master or foreman	18s. per week
2	Picked by women at home	½ d. per pound
3	Oiled by an oiler	9s. per week
4	Willowed by a devil boy	3s. per week
5	Scribbled by an engine boy	3s. per week
6	Carded by an engine boy	3s. per week
7	Slubbed by a jack man	12s. per week
8	Spun by a spinning jenny	Paid by the pound
9	Wound by a woman	6d. to 8d. per pound

(but this pound weighs 5 pound 2 ounces . . . an industrious woman may wind 2 pounds in a day)

10	Warped – irregular work	When full 3s a day
11	Sized by weavers	
12	Weaving – average wage	11s a week
13	Dressing in the fulling mill	Paid by the piece from

4s. to 12s. . . . Earnings from 14s. to 16s. per week.

John Williams, the official measurer of flannel at the Market Hall in his evidence to the Commission, said 'A fair working weaver earns about 12/6 weekly; a middling weaver 9 shillings; and women, children or learners about 6 shillings; subject however to a deduction of one shilling a week for winding and 6 pence a week for candle'.

A factory owner said 'a good weaver is never out of work but the men do not work with the same spirit as formerly . . . I gave

THE LLANIDLOES
WELSH FLANNEL, TWEED,

AND

Woolstapling Company, Limited.

CAPITAL £50,000, in 5,000 Shares of £10 each,

(A large number of which have already been subscribed for.)

Deposit £1 per Share.   Three Months' interval at least will elapse between two Calls, and no Call will exceed £1 per Share.

It is not proposed to call up more than £6 per Share.

DIRECTORS:

HUGH OWEN, Esq., Richmond Crescent, Barnsbury, London.
EDMUND CLEATON, Esq., Vaenor, Llanidloes.
GRIFFITH DAVIES, Esq., Lonsdale Square, London.
GEORGE LEWIS, Esq., Canonbury Park North, London.

BANKERS:

THE NORTH & SOUTH WALES BANK, Llanidloes.
THE LONDON & SOUTH-WESTERN BANK, 27 Regent-Street, London.

SOLICITOR:

EDWARD OSWELL, Esq., Oswestry.

SECRETARY pro tem:

R. C. WALTER, Esq., 155 Fenchurch Street, London, E.C.

TEMPORARY OFFICES—Llanidloes, Montgomeryshire.

[OVER.

Prospectus of a new textile manufacturing company in the 1860s.

work to a man who complained that he could not earn more than 1s. 3d. a day with it. He worked four days and on the fifth went to his potato ground . . . I did put myself into his loom for one day . . . earned me 5 shillings and 5 pence . . . '

The weavers themselves were not so optimistic; one said that he hardly made more than 10 shillings a week and many considered that the average weekly earnings did not exceed 8 shillings and 6 pence. Masters and men were often at variance and a petition presented to the Rev. Evors in his role as magistrate on 1 December, 1838 which 'sheweth that your petitioners do suffer much loss in their earnings by the different impositions practised by the masters . . . First the irregularity in the length of warping walls which are now from four yards eight inches to four yards fourteen inches. Secondly the breadth of the reed which originally was by agreement between masters and men three feet, two inches and a half is now reduced in many factories to three feet only, which caused great injury to the weaver, in respect of his earnings . . . therefore your petitioners humbly pray the breadth to be established three feet, two inches . . . Thirdly your petitioners humbly pray that the number of threads in the warp shall be duly regulated'. This petition was signed by 394 weavers from Newtown.

Throughout the early factory era, the threat from other textile manufacturing districts, particularly the Rochdale district of Lancashire, was a very real one. Even in 1799 when Walter Davies carried out his survey he said, 'An opportunity is here afforded of correcting an error, lately become prevalent in London and several places of confounding the Rochdale stoved white Welsh flannels with the Montgomeryshire real Welsh flannel; while in fact they are very different agreeing neither in length of pieces, in quality of wool nor in the mode of manufacture. The Rochdale flannels never exceed 48 yards a piece, sell from 10_ pence to 2 shillings and 5 pence per yard, have their warp sized in the weaving; and afterwards stoved with brimstone; and owing to their being drawn finer in the thread than the coarseness of the wool will well admit of, they generally appear thread-bare'.

By the time of the visit of the Royal Commission in 1837,

*Demonstration of hand carding by Elaine Williams
at the Weaver's Cottage, Trefriw.*

*Hand spinning with spindle
and whort.*

*Spinning demonstration on a small
'Highland' wheel.*

Hand weaving on a dobby loom at Trefriw Woollen Mill.

Trevor Jones sorting wool   *Weighing fleeces at Trefriw*

*The main 'breast' roller of a carding
engine, Trefriw Woollen Mill.*

*Washing skeins
at Trefriw.*

The dye-house, Trefriw.

Melin Wlân Trefriw – the old buildings.

The new building at Trefriw which includes interpretive exhibition, shop, cafe and power house.

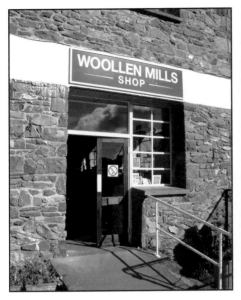

Shop entrance, Trefriw.

Trevor Jones carding – intermedials feed.

Old mill buildings on the banks of Afon Crafnant – the river once provided water wheel power for driving machinery

Self-acting mule for spinning

Winding from cop to cone

Working the self-acting mule at Trefriw.

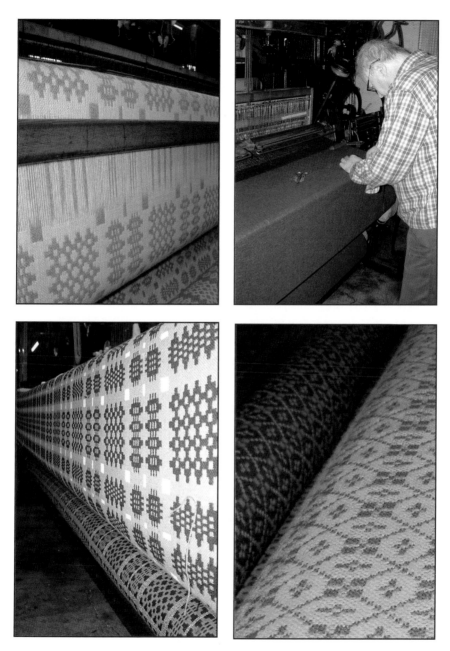

Woven carthenni *on Dobcross looms at Trefriw.*

The products at Trefriw's retail shop

*Alison Cull measuring
and cutting cloth*

A variety of textiles for sale at Trefriw Woollen Mill.

Ffatri Penmachno – now disused.

*The old factory shop in
Penmachno village.*

*Melin Bryncir retail shop,
Y Maes, Caernarfon*

Water wheel,
Melin Bryncir

Mill leat,
Rock Mills, Capel Dewi, Llandysul

A 24' water wheel at Melin Pant-yr-ynn, Blaenau Ffestiniog.

Melin Wlân Bryncir

A Great Wheel at Bryncir

*Carding engine, still in use
at Melin Bryncir*

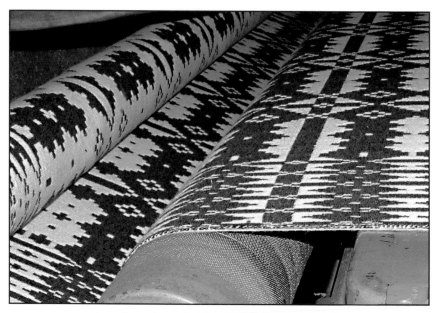

A variety of patterns produced at Melin Bryncir.

Warp mill at Curlew Weavers, Troed-yr-aur, Ceredigion

Carding engine, Curlew Weavers

Tremadog Mills, where the first steam driven machines in Wales were installed.

Pontyweli Mill, Llandysul – now a confectionery store.

Derw Mill, Pentre-cwrt, Llandysul. Once one of the largest of the Dyffryn Teifi mills, now a furniture workshop.

Pant-yr-ynn mill at Blaenau Ffestiniog – now an art gallery.

*Woolpack Inn,
Dyffryn Ceiriog*

*Upper Mills, Glynceiriog –
now a fine furniture workshop.*

Melin Meirion, Dinas Mawddwy – now a retail shop and craft centre.

*Gareth Jenkins demonstrating the craft of the hand weaver at Esgair Moel mill,
now at the Museum of Welsh Life, St Fagans.*

Rochdale flannel was a very real competitor for although 'there is not substance or weight equal to the Welsh . . . the pieces look fine and good to the eye, and take in the market'. Later in the century, the popularity of Rochdale flannel was a factor contributing to the disappearance of the industry from Montgomeryshire.

The report of the Royal Commission gives a fairly comprehensive picture of life in Newtown in the late eighteen-thirties. It described how a co-operative society was established in 1832 'in order to amass capital to employ ourselves' said one weaver. A general store was established, but by 1838 the business had failed 'by the dishonesty of the storekeeper who ran away to America with money. A field was rented by this Society . . . each member paid a rent in proportion to the size and situation of his garden . . . the object being to better the condition of the members, which it actually did; one of the members with a wife and four children, who were out of work during the winter were enabled to live upon the produce of the bit of land'. Gardening was considered an important supplementary source of income for the weavers: 'Almost all the poor people set potatoes in the fallow of the neighbouring farmers paying a ground rent of ten shillings for every strike of potatoes they may set. The strike is eight bowls, each bowl weighing 24 pounds . . . the farmer manures and prepares the ground . . . They also rent small allotment gardens at the rent of £12 per acre . . . nearly all keep pigs . . . when waiting for work they employ themselves in their gardens'.

Life in the town in the eighteen-thirties was difficult; poverty was rife and 'weavers marry young and die young'. There was no daily school for the children of the poor. 'By the introduction of the Factory Act,' said one observer, 'numbers of the children were deprived of employment, their parents being poor and unable to give them education, they roam the streets in vice and ignorance . . . they remain under the roof of their parents, and brought up in the manufacturing business, overstock the trade with hands'. Conditions in Newtown were such that the town was a seed bed of discontent and Chartism: 'the great revolutionary movement of the working classes, produced a response from the radical tradesmen and the skilled and unskilled operatives in the flannel towns of the

Severn valley'. Already in 1830, local riots in protest at low wages had caused the hasty reforming of the Montgomeryshire Yeomanry and the enrolment of hundreds of special constables. The first Chartist meeting in Wales was held in Newtown on 3 October, 1838 and this meeting, addressed by the well-known reformer Charles Jones of Welshpool, was attended by 4,000 people. There followed a year of unprecedented violence, with the textile workers of Newtown and Llanidloes in the forefront of every demonstration. The headquarters of the movement was the village of Mochdre, a mile from Newtown, which at that time was a centre of the weaving and fulling industries.

The industry in northern and central Wales

Eclipse 1850-1870

'The flannel trade is in about the most unsatisfactory a condition as it can be, the high price of raw material and the small demand and low prices for the manufactured article making it a losing business. It is not too much to say that excepting some change comes, a large number of workmen will be out of employ' (*Montgomery Express*, 1873). Things were difficult in the Montgomeryshire flannel industry in the 1840s and 1850s. Much of the flannel was still produced on hand-looms and amongst masters and weavers there was a marked reluctance to adopt the power loom, that was already in use by the thousand in the north of England. The most forward looking of Newtown weaving masters, the Rev. William Pugh made an attempt to introduce the power loom to the town, but his efforts were not appreciated and he had to flee the country in disgrace loaded with debts.

In the meantime, the wool textile industry in the north of England was prospering and the modern factories of Rochdale and Huddersfield were producing ever-increasing quantities of fabrics and saturating the market with cheaply-produced flannel. Something had to be done and in the 1850s and 1860s the Montgomeryshire manufacturers woke up to the fact that they had to modernize their industry if they were to survive. New, large mill

Pryce Jones' Royal Welsh Warehouse.
The first mail-order business in the world.

buildings were constructed in Newtown and Llanidloes; new machinery was installed; new steam engines to power those machines were purchased and new companies were floated, in an attempt 'to stay the exodus of the Welsh flannel trade to the north of England'. But even the largest and most modern of Montgomeryshire mills was a minnow compared with some of the vast undertakings of Lancashire and Yorkshire, yet, so much capital was tied up in plant and equipment that factory owners had little money left to run their mills. The vast Severn Valley Mills alongside the railway line at Newtown, for example, were built in the early 1870s and fully equipped with the most modern steam-driven equipment then available. Before a yard of cloth was woven, the owner of the mills found himself in deep financial troubles and was declared bankrupt. The mill was never used except as a wool warehouse and small shawl factory.

Pryce Jones

Although a great deal of capital was invested in the woollen industry in the 1850s and 1860s, although new machinery was bought and companies amalgamated, the modernization programme came too late to save the industry from extinction. Oddly enough there was a short-lived revival in the early seventies, that made the most optimistic of newspaper correspondents speak again of 'Newtown – the Leeds of Wales'. That revival came about as the result of the efforts of one person – Pryce Jones who established the first mail-order business in the whole world in Newtown. 'The humdrum routine of the old style of conducting the business', wrote his biographer, 'was but little congenial to his ideas, which thus early yearned for a more extended field of operation and his enterprises felt that it could not be bounded by his native mountains. Thereupon he commenced that system of business which was then quite unique. Pryce Jones thought that the public should be brought into more direct contact with the producer . . . He therefore commenced by sending patterns to a few of the gentry in his own immediate neighbourhood and the surrounding districts and the circle thus started has gone on increasing until he claims as clients some 100,000 patrons'. From a small shop near the market hall, Pryce Jones moved his business to a new building near the railway station, completed in 1879 and extended in 1895. At the warehouse he employed over 300 people and goods were sent by post to all parts of the world. The early prosperity of Pryce Jones' business was based almost entirely on Welsh flannel. As the catalogue for 1887 notes, 'Pryce Jones in appealing to the Ladies of England to support native industries . . . has after mature thought come to the determination of supplying in future to his numerous patrons, Goods which are exclusively of home manufacture', and he supplied 'Real Welsh Flannel direct from the looms, Gentlemen's Welsh Tweeds, Shawls, Blankets, Hosiery and sterling value clothing for the poor'. These flannels were made at one of the textile mills that Pryce Jones operated in Newtown and Welshpool, while shawls, hosiery and ready-made clothes were manufactured at one of the factories in Newtown. So great did the trade become

Pryce Jones' catalogue of 1887.

that 'the London and North West Railway Company have built and run specially for Mr Jones' traffic, three luggage carriages divided into compartments for the more ready distribution of parcels at the several centres of distribution along their lines. Each of their vans is labelled with Mr Jones' name, business and location and run daily to and from Newtown and Euston'.

Nevertheless, despite the temporary revival brought about as a result of the growth of the mail order business, Pryce Jones' enterprise failed to save the Sir Drefaldwyn woollen industry from extinction, for although the business flourished, the amount of local flannel sold became less and less. Pryce Jones extended his business to sell goods, other than flannel, but he found it more economical to buy 'Real Welch flannel' in Rochdale and transport it by rail to his Royal Welsh Warehouse for redistribution to his customers.

Reasons for the decline of the Montgomeryshire flannel industry

1.   The flannel makers attempted to compete with the north or England manufacturers on their own terms, producing the same range of goods but far less efficiently. There was little to distinguish Montgomeryshire flannel from that produced in Yorkshire and Lancashire. The Montgomeryshire manufacturers also attempted to enter the fancy textile trade producing such things as shawls and scarves that were already being produced far more cheaply and in sufficient quantities by the northern industry. It was an impossible market for a late entrant.

2.   If the industry was to succeed, capital should have been invested in new plants and buildings in the 1830s and 1840s, not in the 1860s. In the forties, flannel was in world-wide demand, but antiquated methods of production and lack of organization meant that Sir Drefaldwyn could not take advantage of favourable conditions at the time.

3.   No investor was prepared to risk his money in a Chartist-ridden industry that was characterized by constant confrontations between master and weaver. This was particularly true in the early 1840s.

4. The modernization programme came far too late to succeed, for the market was already dominated by more efficient industrialists. When the Montgomeryshire industry was finally modernized it had very little to offer that was different or better.
5. The Shropshire canal that reached Newtown in 1824 and the railway system later on, ran from west to east rather than from north to south. The transport facilities brought the mass-produced materials of the industrial north and midlands to the heart of Wales and those regions were not good for the sale of Welsh cloth. If the rail had led to the south it would have brought the ever-growing valleys of industrial southern Wales within reach of the Montgomeryshire flannel industry. Indeed the existence of that vast market brought a new prosperity to another textile manufacturing district – that of the Teifi valley in western Wales.
6. Montgomeryshire was too far away from the coalfields and the cost of transporting coal by rail or canal to the factories to run the steam engines was prohibitive.

By 1870 the Montgomeryshire woollen manufacturer was faced with competition on all sides: his industry was neither technologically or economically sound; his products were not in world wide demand and he failed to meet the challenge of changing fashion. Slowly, trade diminished and by the end of the

The end of an era – the aftermath of a fire at Cambrian Mills, Newtown, 1912.

Meirionnydd

The industry in Meirionnydd was considerably smaller than in Montgomeryshire . In Meirionnydd, the web industry throughout its history remained a widely scattered rural industry and Dolgellau and Bala never became centres of manufacture like Newtown and Llanidloes. As in Sir Drefaldwyn the establishment of fulling mills marked the first stage in the transference of the woollen industry from homestead to factory and Meirionnydd with its multiplicity of swiftly flowing streams was well adapted by nature for the establishment of fulling mills. The first reference to fulling mills was in 1545 when Maes-y-Pandy near Dolgellau is mentioned in a legal document. Between 1545 and 1700 at least thirty-eight pandai were build in the county, with a further thirty established between 1700 and 1810. In some cases fulling mills were accommodated in already existing corn mills and one person would carry out the tasks of corn milling and fulling in a single building. In other cases many fullers were part-time farmers and the pandai were integral parts of farmsteads.

Again carding, spinning and weaving were exclusively domestic crafts until the end of the eighteenth century; indeed they remained a part of the domestic routine of Meirionnydd homes for as long as textile manufacturing was practised on any scale in the county. 'Almost every little farmer make webs', writes Arthur Aikin in 1797, 'and few cottages in these parts are without a loom.' Meirionnydd weavers had by the mid-eighteenth century gained a considerable reputation as good craftsmen. It is difficult to ascertain whether this reputation was fully deserved, but Idris Fychan in his History of Dolgellau considered the quality of Meirionnydd cloth as being much better than Sir Drefaldwyn flannel and that at the Shrewsbury cloth market the prices paid for Dolgellau webs were higher than those paid for any other cloth produced in Wales.

It was only very slowly that water-driven machinery was adopted by Meirionnydd manufacturers; the first carding engine being introduced into a fulling mill at Mallwyd in 1798 and another to a mill at Pennal in 1799. Both these mills were on the southern

Upper Mills, Glynceiriog, Denbighshire

periphery of the county and in close proximity to Sir Drefaldwyn, and it was not until 1801 that carding engines made an appearance in the Dolgellau district. Between 1798 and 1815 some fifty-two carding and spinning mills were established in the county; the majority being established in already existing fulling or corn mills. During the first quarter of the nineteenth century, therefore, carding and spinning became a factory industry in Meirionnydd but an appreciable amount of domestic, hand carding and spinning persisted until the last quarter of the nineteenth century. It was only the more substantial farmers that could afford to send their wool for processing to factories, and cottagers still depended on domestic spinners. Stocking knitting was, of course, as important as weaving in eastern Meirionnydd and the knitters had to be supplied with yarn, mainly spun in the cottages of the county.

During the 1820s, a number of Meirionnydd carding and spinning mills installed hand looms, but the amount of cloth woven on these looms was limited, for the mills even as late as 1850 were still concerned with supplying yarn for domestic weavers and knitters. For example the account books of Ffrydan mill, Bala show that in 1845, 4,010½ lb. of wool was processed at the mill, but only 642 lb. of this was made up into blankets or cloth at the mill itself.

As in Montgomeryshire the eighteen thirties and forties was a period of difficulty for the Meirionnydd textile manufacturer, but the decline in Meirionnydd was not as spectacular as it was in Montgomeryshire. Little capital was invested in Meirionnydd mills; indeed most of the mill owners were part-time farmers. Manufacturers set limits to their production and marketing; many of the mills could be worked single handed and they were never dependent on changeable export markets. Neither did the Meirionnydd mill owners adopt the panic measure of Montgomeryshire by buying power-driven machinery, when they were not in a position to pay for it. By 1840, therefore, the Meirionnydd industry gradually ceased to be of importance; it ceased to resemble the flannel industry of Montgomeryshire and became instead an industry concerned with supplying the needs of self-sufficing local communities, and was no more important than the woollen industry in Ynys Môn, Sir Gaernarfon and Sir Faesyfed (*Radnorshire*).

The development of the woollen trade in neighbouring Denbighshire was similar to that in Meirionnydd. The product was similar but the industry was considerably smaller being concentrated in the Ceiriog valley. It was largely a domestic industry dependent on a large number of domestic spinners and individual weavers who took their products for finishing to one of the eleven fulling mills in the valley. Some of those fulling mills became fully comprehensive mills where all the processes of textile manufacture were concentrated during the first decade of the nineteenth century, and as such one large mill was in production until the late nineteen fifties.

Water power from a mountain stream at Pant-yr-ynn, Blaenau Ffestiniog, Gwynedd.

The rural industry

The woollen industry in the Severn valley and to a lesser extent in Meirionnydd and Denbighshire, was a highly competitive, specialized industry concerned very largely with the export of its products outside the immediate region of production. Montgomeryshire flannel clothed the armies of the Duke of Wellington and the slaves of North America; the manufacturers were in direct competition with the industrialists of the north of

A rural mill at Llanrhystud, Ceredigion.

England and most of them made an effort to buy the most modern textile machinery available at any one time. But there was also another side to the story of the Welsh woollen industry, for the untroubled waters of the rural manufacturer had little in common with the turmoil of the Newtown and Llanidloes industrialist. Throughout rural Wales there were domestic weavers and owners of small mills that were concerned with supplying a local market. To those craftsmen, as essential to the community as the village cobbler or wheelwright, the cut-throat world of international marketing did not exist, for the rural weaver's customers were his own neighbours. After shearing in the summer, farmers would take their wool to the local mill with an order for knitting yarn and lengths of flannel, blankets and tweed for the use of the farmer and his family. Quite often no money payment was involved at all, for the mill owner kept a proportion of all the fleeces brought in by farmers as his payment. At the Cwm Isaf Mill, Mynachlog-ddu in Pembrokeshire, for example, the owner of the mill set aside a tenth of all the fleeces brought in for processing by Preseli farmers. This was then made up into cloth or blankets to be sold at a market stall in Haverfordwest or Crymych.

Many of the rural woollen manufacturers were farmers themselves, who were only able to devote time to woollen manufacturing at slack times in the farming year. W. P. Crankshaw, of Salford Technical College who carried out a survey of the Welsh woollen industry in the nineteen twenties, was very surprised to see woollen mills that accommodated butter churns, cheese presses and even cattle and was even more surprised when he visited one mill to see a woollen manufacturer appearing with a scythe on his shoulder and was greeted with 'Come again another day as I have two men in the field and cannot leave them'.

The Esgair Moel Woollen Mill re-erected at the Museum of Welsh Life is typical of the small rural mills that at one time dotted the Welsh countryside. The mill from Llanwrtyd in Powys was built about 1760, and from about 1880 until it finally closed in 1947 the mill was operated by Isaac Williams and his son Rees who ran it in conjunction with a farm. The factory, a long, whitewashed stone building is typical of the all-purpose rural woollen mill that sprang up in most parts of Wales in the late eighteenth and early

A rural mill – the Esgair Moel mill, Llanwrtyd, Powys now at the Museum of Welsh Life, St. Fagans.

nineteenth centuries. In it, all the processes of textile manufacture from dyeing the raw material to fulling and pressing the finished cloth were carried out. The customers of the mill were those people who attended the Builth market where Isaac Williams set up his weekly stall. They came from all over Radnorshire, and as far south as the Epynt and Carmarthenshire borders and as far eastwards as the Radnor Forest. Farmers brought their wool at shearing time to the market stall; they placed orders for cloth, bedclothes and knitting yarn and collected finished products from the stall. It was a haphazard business and delivery of orders could take many months.

Woollen mill, Tal-y-bont, Ceredigion, 1936

Dre-fach Felindre – a textile village

As the industry declined in Powys during the second half of the nineteenth century, it enjoyed a period of unprecedented prosperity in rural western Wales. The villages of Teifi-side – Henllan, Llandysul and Dre-fach, became the most important of manufacturing centres. The twin villages of Dre-fach Felindre and the adjacent hamlets of Waungilwern, Drefelin, Cwmhiraeth and Cwmpengraig were by far the most important of these textile villages, and most of the inhabitants were concerned with some aspect of textile manufacture. Most of them worked in one of the local mills, but others were concerned with weaving in their own homes. Many too, were engaged as 'outworkers' making up shirts, shawls and underwear for one or other of the mills. By 1900, Dre-fach Felindre had developed to such an extent that a local historian could write:

There are no parishes in Wales possibly, that produce more Welsh flannel than the two parishes (Llangeler and Penboyr). Nearly all the power of the streams and rivers has been harnessed to drive machinery. There is hardly a spot on the banks of rivers where it would be convenient to build an additional factory or mill.

Why Dre-fach?

In 1837 the Royal Commission on Handloom Weavers visited Wales, but they did not consider western Wales worthy of a visit. Yet, by 1900 the Teifi valley was by far the most important textile manufacturing region in the country. The development was almost fortuitous, for it is virtually impossible to point to any one factor why a remote, rural valley should have become a centre of industrial development. Undoubtedly one of the factors that contributed to the development of the woollen industry in the Teifi valley was the availability of water to drive machinery and to scour and wash raw wool and fabrics. Many of the mills were built on the south side of the Teifi, where swiftly flowing streams such as the Bargod, Esger and Siedi fall into the main river to provide a plentiful supply of water. The textile villages too were in close proximity to the sheep farms of the lower hill slopes of western

Domestic textile workers at Dre-fach Felindre, Carmarthenshire c. 1875.

Wales, so that there was a plentiful supply of raw material for the industry within the region itself. The villages were also within reasonable reach of the industrial valleys of southern Wales and when the railway reached Pencader in 1864 and Castellnewydd Emlyn in 1895, it provided the means of taking the products of the industry to its main market in southern Wales. The evidence suggests that well before the heyday of the industry there was already a great deal of expertise in the region, especially in spinning and the preparation of yarn. At the turn of the nineteenth century, the woollen trade was given considerable encouragement by the Carmarthenshire Agricultural Society who offered five annual premiums 'to cottagers who shall spin the greatest quantity of yarn from the first day of January to the end of the same year'. Every year for as long as the scheme operated all the prizes were won by women from the Dre-fach district. Domestic stocking knitters and a number of specialized hand-loom weavers, who worked at looms in their own homes, utilized the spun yarn produced by the women on their spinning wheels. The cloth could

Dolwion Mill, Dre-fach Felindre. A mill that started as a fulling mill.

be taken to one of the four fulling mills in the district, to Pentre-cwrt, Dolwion, Cwmpengraig or Felindre, and then sold locally or at markets in the region. In 1871 there were 104 specialized domestic weavers in the Dre-fach district. Many were smallholders and some of the most prosperous employed one or two weavers.

Mechanisation

Although hand-loom weavers continued to operate in the district well into the twentieth century, the greatest innovation was the introduction of power looms into the industry after about 1880. The region entered a period of unprecedented prosperity that continued unabated until the early nineteen twenties. Mills were built and the industry attracted labour from other areas, not only to work in the textile industry, but also to actually build mill buildings. Of course, there were in existence a few mills for carding, spinning and fulling well before 1880, but it was only after that date that the movement from homestead to factory gathered pace. As early as 1810, carding machinery in the form of a water-driven scribbler-carder was introduced into a fulling mill at Cwmpengraig. In the 1820s its owner installed a spinning jack of 40 spindles into the same building. This mill, known as Coedmor, continued as a carding, spinning and fulling mill until 1878, when it was rebuilt by John Phillips as a fully comprehensive mill.

Another mill, Dolwion, also began as a fulling mill and both carding and spinning machinery was introduced into the mill in the 1820s.

Not all the early nineteenth century mills were incorporated in already existing pandai. Llwynbedw, later to become Dyffryn Mills, was built especially by John Lewis around 1835 as a carding, spinning and weaving mill. It contained scribbler and condenser carders, a partly water-driven mule of 120 spindles and a number of hand looms. According to the census of 1871, Samuel Williams, whose family had owned the mill from about 1845, employed 20 men and women and 3 boys. Of these, three were spinners, one was a carder and the remainder were weavers. Samuel Williams was a pioneer of textile manufacturing in the district and for many years he was the leading figure on the committee that periodically

*Cafan Bridge Mills, later Alltcafan Mill, Pentre-cwrt, Llandysul. A mill built
in 1895 and regarded as one of the most modern in Wales when it was built.*

drew up the price and wages list for weavers. He was one of the
first to produce textiles right through from the initial sorting of
wool to finishing. His example was soon followed by other mill
owners with the result that the specialized fulling mills closed or
ceased to specialize and domestic spinning virtually disappeared.
The introduction of spinning machinery brought severe discontent
to the hand spinners of Dre-fach Felindre, especially when the first
'jacks' were introduced in the eighteen twenties and thirties. But as
more machinery was introduced and as those machines became
increasingly larger in size, there was very little that the
independent spinster could do except accept the situation. It is
significant that in 1871, when the writing was already on the wall
for the domestic spinner, that the average age of the women
employed in the trade was as high as 64 years of age, compared
with an average age for hand loom weavers of 39 years. In the
declining years of hand-spinning, only the elderly still clung to a
trade that was being superceded at a rapid rate by more modern

power-driven equipment. The hand-loom weavers held on a little longer, although by 1900 most of them were employed as weavers in factories.

During the last quarter of the nineteenth century, the Dre-fach Felindre district entered a period of prosperity, a large proportion of the trade being aimed at the mining and metallurgical valleys of southern Wales. Certain mills concentrated on certain areas and mill owners had long standing agreements with drapers in southern Wales industrial towns. For example, Pantybarcud mills sent much of their product to drapers in Maesteg, Aberdare and Port Talbot, while flannel produced at Pantglas mill, Cwmhiraeth, was sent to the Gwent and Rhondda valleys in particular.

With the development of the industry between 1890 and 1914, machinery, often second-hand machinery from Yorkshire mills, was purchased by the textile manufacturers. Ben Jones of Ogof Factory, for example, when he decided to convert his weaving shop to a fully comprehensive mill, built a new building across the road from the old weaving shop. This was equipped with a 48 inch scribbler and carder to produce 24 good threads, a hand mule of 240 spindles, a 44 inch power loom and three 38 inch power looms. John Jones of Bargod Mills equipped his new mill building about 1890 with a 48 inch carding engine producing 20 threads, hand mule of 200 spindles, two 45 inch and one 40 inch power looms. The arrival of the railway at nearby Henllan in 1895 provided the impetus for a rapid development of the industry. The large Alltcafan Mills at Pentre-cwrt, originally called the Cafan Bridge Mills, were built in close proximity to the railway in the late nineties and smaller factories like Llainffald in Felindre were built and enlarged and became something more than mere weaving sheds. Whereas before, these mills were dependent on yarn carded and spun in specialized yarn factories or by domestic spinners, they now installed power machinery to deal with all processes of textile manufacture.

The toll of prosperity

By 1900, prosperity reigned in Dre-fach Felindre, so that a contemporary observer could write: 'The unhealthy and smoke-

68

Tom Rees weaving a 'tapestry' quilt at Maesllyn Mill, Ceredigion in 1968.
The industry in late 19th century western Wales was dependent
on power looms of this type

filled cottages have disappeared and beautiful new houses have been built every-where. Craftsmen in many trades are more numerous and in constant work; the rateable value of the houses is so great that the burden on farmers has been lightened.' It was a short-lived prosperity which did not really begin until about 1880, but was to end shortly after the end of the First World War. During that period of about forty years, there was a constant demand for the products of the looms – fortunes were amassed by the owners of mils who could call on an adequate supply of labour. In such villages as Dre-fach, Pentre-cwrt and Llandysul, children soon followed their parents to work in the textile mills; indeed, mill owners expected that the children of their employees should work at the textile factories, even before their schooldays were over. For example, children in the Cwm Morgan district were expected to work at one of the local mills as soon as they were ten years of age, mainly to look after carding engines. The hours of work were from five until eight in the evening for which they were paid three-pence an evening in 1907. In addition they were expected to work on Saturday mornings from 8 a.m. until 1 p.m. for which they were paid fourpence. As soon as schooldays were over, children were expected to become full-time employees at one of the mills. Apprenticeship as a textile worker lasted for three years and it was customary in western Wales to have one apprentice to every four experienced workmen. During the first years, the apprentice did nothing at all except look after the carding engines and in the early years of the twentieth century he was paid at the rate of ten pence a day for a six-day week. The working day lasted for twelve hours, the workers either starting at 7 a.m. or 8 a.m. Around 1907, when it became customary to work a five-and-a-half-day week, some of the workers were still expected to work at the factories for six full days. Dyeing and washing, where little machinery was required and there was therefore no noise, was the usual task performed on Saturday afternoons, despite the fact that Inspectors of Factories paid frequent visits to the mills to make sure that no young people were employed after 1 p.m. on Saturdays. Moreover, the women were expected to take shawls and blankets to their homes for hemming and fringing over the weekend.

In the 1900s there was considerable discontent in the factories of the middle Teifi valley, in that mill owners refused to start paying their employees until the end of the working week at 1 p.m. on Saturdays. Payment of wages was often not completed until 3 p.m. The wages paid to experienced workers were not high. Spinners were paid at the rate of 18s. per week, rising to a maximum of 25s. after some five years' service. Weavers on the other hand were paid a piece-rate wage, ranging from 1d. to 18d., according to the factory. Within each factory, except the smallest, there was a distinct division of labour, for in addition to spinners and weavers, other people were required for carding, dyeing, fulling and finishing.

"The Burning City" – fire at the Dyffryn Mills, Felindre, 1923.

Eclipse 1918-1925

The woollen industry, with its dependence on the industrial market of southern Wales, flourished until the end of the First World War; indeed, during the period 1914-18 the price of wool reached a record level. The end of the war spelt disaster to the industry. The price of wool fell from 4s. 6d. a pound to 9d. a pound within the space of a few months. This was a fall that the small mills could not face and dozens were forced to close down. The consequences of this situation were reflected in the condition and appearance of the countryside. Improvements to dwellings were at a standstill, buildings decayed and many were completely abandoned. Bankruptcy faced many mill owners and all were preoccupied with the task of making ends meet. Weavers were dismissed because wages could not be paid, and there was a wholesale exodus to the towns and industrial regions. Chapels, grocery stores, public houses and craft workshops closed by the

The day after the disastrous fire at Cambrian Mills, Dre-fach Felindre, 1919.

dozen and organizations such as choirs, dramatic societies and brass bands ceased to exist. During the decade 1918-28 fourteen of the factories experienced disastrous fires and only two were rebuilt. In Dre-fach Felindre alone out of a total of fifty mills in 1900, at least twenty ceased to function in the period immediately following the First World War.

Henry and Howard at the mill door, Melin Tregwynt, Pembrokeshire.

Working the machines at Melin Tregwynt, Pembrokeshire.

Rock Mills, Capel Dewi, Llandysul

Cambrian Factory, Llanwrtyd, Powys

Elvet Mills, Cynwyl Elfed, Carmarthenshire

The Woollen Industry Today

The woollen industry in Wales today is represented by no more than 10 mills compared with nearly 90 in 1945. Those that remain at work today, in western Wales and Gwynedd in particular, are remnants of a much more intensive pattern of distribution. Until the nineteen thirties, small, comprehensive mills were vital to the economy of many a rural community. Some of the mills in production in Wales today originated in the old self-sufficing communities of rural Wales, for although mills such as Tregwynt at St Nicholas in Pembrokeshire and the Bryncir mill at Golan in Gwynedd are very dependent on a tourist industry as a source of revenue, they like many others started off as essential elements in the self-sufficing pattern of community life.

Some of the other mills in production in Wales today had a somewhat different origin. They represent the remnants of one of the most important of native Welsh industries, concerned not so much with a local market, but with an extensive international one. It is in the Teifi valley in Carmarthenshire and Ceredigion that the

Cambrian Mills, Dre-fach, Felindre. The mills were built in 1912 and now house the National Woollen Museum

industry still flourishes on a greatly diminished scale and the few mills in that area are the remnants of a golden era in the history of rural Wales.

The most depressing feature of the post-1945 period in the history of the woollen industry has been the decline in the number of mills. The number of people engaged in the industry has also declined alarmingly. It does not seem that the trend has abated in any way. Large modernized mills as well as small one-man businesses have closed by the dozen and although the market for Welsh cloth was extended with the introduction of double-woven tapestry cloths, furnishing fabrics and light flannels to replace the traditional shawls, shirts and flannel drawers, the number of craftsmen supplying that demand has declined alarmingly. Those that remain in the industry are now heavily dependent on the seasonal tourist market.

One of the reason for the decline of the industry since 1945 has been the difficulty experienced by mill owners in recruiting labour, for almost all Welsh mills employ far fewer staff than they did in the past. Wages in the woollen industry compare unfavourably with those paid in other occupations, while in most of the mills there has been a marked reluctance to invest in new capital equipment. Some mills have been modernized, but the majority have become dependent on dyed yarn produced by Yorkshire yarn producers and have been reduced to the status of specialized weaving mills, unconcerned with such vital processes as carding, spinning and cloth finishing. Another trend of the period 1950-75 has been the difficulty of selling woollen mills as going concerns. When factory owners have wished to retire they have experienced great difficulty in selling and, for this reason alone, many have ceased production.

By tradition, the Welsh woollen industry is a producer of flannel which in the past not only clothed the miners of southern Wales but also the slaves of north America. Although mills still produce flannel, designed mainly for the fashion industry, the characteristic product of the Welsh woollen industry between 1950 and 1975 was double-woven 'tapestry' cloth and bedcovers. The origins of this multi-coloured, patterned material are obscure, but

Melin Dolwerdd, Cwmpengraig

it seems that in the eighteenth century some intricate patterns were woven on hand-looms in north-eastern Wales. Tapestry material was as well-known in Scotland, in Kentucky, in north-west Canada and amongst the Indian tribes of the United States of America and there is nothing to indicate that this material, so often associated with Wales in recent years, was ever a part of the Welsh craft tradition; indeed before the nineteen thirties, tapestry was hardly known in Wales except in a few mills in the north. Like the honeycomb quilt of the nineteen forties, it seems that the market for tapestry is in decline and perhaps a reversion to flannel and the development of new fabrics may be necessary for the revival of our most important of Welsh rural industries.

Today that once important industry is represented by less than a dozen mills mainly in the tourist areas of Wales. Only one or two of these mills are concerned with all the processes of production, for yarn for weaving is usually bought in other regions and other countries. Only the remnants of a once important industry remain.

Raymond Jones of Melin Teifi operating in a part of the old Cambrian Mills, Dre-fach Felindre, now the National Woollen Museum.

Early exhibitions at the National Woollens Museum

TEXTILE PRODUCTION 2005

Melin Tregwynt, Castle Morris, Haverfordwest, Pembrokeshire
Melin Teifi, Cambrian Mills, Dre-fach Felindre, Carmarthenshire
(on the premises of the National Woollen Museum)
Melin Dolwerdd, Cwmpengraig, Dre-fach Felindre
Curlew Weavers, Troed-yr-aur, Rhydlewis, Ceredigion
Esgair Moel Mill, Museum of Welsh Life, St Fagans, Caerdydd
Rock Mills, Capel Dewi, Llandysul, Ceredigion
Middle Mill, Solfach, Pembrokeshire
Elvet Mills, Cynwyl Elfed, Carmarthenshire
Cambrian Factory, Llanwrtyd Wells, Powys
Trefriw Woollen Mills, Trefriw, Sir Conwy
Bryncir Woollen Mill, Golan, Garndolbenmaen, Gwynedd

There are a number of weaving shops, usually operated by one or two artist craftsmen in many parts of Wales. Some of these only operate on a temporary or seasonal basis. Also yarn producers, such as The Natural Fibre Company, Llanbedr Pont Steffan.

In addition to the National Woollen Museum at Dre-fach Felindre, Carmarthenshire and the Esgair Moel mill at the the Museum of Welsh Life at St Fagans, Caerdydd, a number of old mills have been adapted for other purposes. For instance, Derw Mill is a fine furniture workshop and the Wallis Mill, Ambleston, Pembrokeshire produces furnishings. Others, like the Meirion Mill, Dinas Mawddwy, Gwynedd are now craft shops, and are still concerned with the interpretation of the industry. In Powys, the Newtown Textile Museum, housed in an early nineteenth century weaving factory interprets the woollen trade in Powys.

Power loom at Melin Teifi, Cambrian Mills, Dre-fach Felindre.

MELIN TEIFI

Cambrian Mill, Museum of the Welsh Woollen Industry,
Dre-fach Felindre, Llandysul SA44 5UP
Tel: 01559 370929   www.nmgw.ac.uk/mwwi/
Open: April – September, 7 days a week and limited hours during the winter;
admission free.

Craftsmen can still be seen working the machines, treating the wool and weaving fabrics within the old mill which is now a national centre for the whole industry in Wales. Also on the site is a research and collection centre, education facilities, coffee shop and picnic area, products shop, facilities for the disabled, car parking.

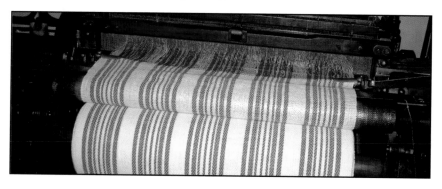

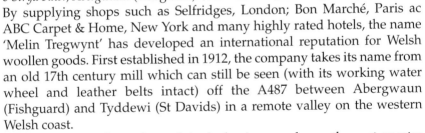

MELIN TREGWYNT

Castle Morris, Hwlffordd (Haverfordwest),
Sir Benfro (Pembrokeshire), *SA62 5UX.*
Tel: 01348 891225
(Orders by post: 01348 891644)
e-mail: info@melintregwynt.co.uk   website: www.melintregwynt.co.uk
Also at: 26 Royal Arcade, Caerdydd (Cardiff), *CF10 1AE. (02920 224997)*
6 Stryd Fawr, Abergwaun (Fishguard). *(01348 872370)*
By supplying shops such as Selfridges, London; Bon Marché, Paris ac
ABC Carpet & Home, New York and many highly rated hotels, the name
'Melin Tregwynt' has developed an international reputation for Welsh
woollen goods. First established in 1912, the company takes its name from
an old 17th century mill which can still be seen (with its working water
wheel and leather belts intact) off the A487 between Abergwaun
(Fishguard) and Tyddewi (St Davids) in a remote valley on the western
Welsh coast.

Over 20 local people work in the business and over the past quarter
century, much emphasis has been placed on colourful designs and giving
a modern style to classic traditional products.

Admission free to the old mill; coffee shop and mill shop open 7
days a week. Melin Tregwynt also has a mail-order catalogue and goods
can now be purchased on their website as well.

TREFRIW WOOLLEN MILLS

Trefriw, Conwy, LL27 ONQ.
Tel: 01492 640462; www.t-w-m.co.uk; e-mail: info@t-w-m.co.uk
Open all year; parking nearby, admission free.

Trefriw Woollen Mills on the banks of Afon Crafnant is still owned and run by the descendants of Thomas Williams who bought the mill in 1859. It was originally a 'pandy' (fulling mill) to which local people brought their cloth to be washed and shrunk in the soft waters, which were also used to drive two water wheels. In 1900, turbines replaced the old water wheels and in 1952 a new dam was built a quarter of a mile upstream. The water flows down a steel pipe to generate electricity to power the mill's machinery. Weaving and hydro-electric turbines can be viewed all year (Mon-Fri). The shop offers own products – bedspreads, tweeds, travelling rugs and garments and accessories made from fabrics woven at the mill. It also stocks pure wool knitwear and sheepskin products. There is also a coffee shop on the premises, hand spinning and hand weaving exhibitions and the main mill machinery rooms are open to the public from Easter onwards (please telephone for hours). Across the yard, the weaver's garden grows all kinds of plants used to treat and dye wool.

CURLEW WEAVERS (GWEHYDDION Y GYLFINIR)

Troedyraur, Rhydlewis, Ceredigion, SA44 5RL.
Tel/Ffacs: 01239 851357   website: westwales.co.uk/curlew.htm
Open all year round, Monday-Friday, 9 a.m.-5 p.m., closed on bank holidays.

Curlew Weavers is a small family firm situated mid-way between Llangrannog and Castellnewydd Emlyn (Newcastle Emlyn) in Ceredigion. It specialises in producing a wide range of woollen fabrics for curtain and upholstery for homes, hotels, boats and caravans.

It also produces lighter fabrics for clothes, bedspreads, tablecloths, baby blankets, shawls, etc.

The shop on the site stocks a good selection of Welsh produce; also bargain-priced knitting wools. There are free tours around the mill, access for disabled. Demonstrations by appointment; coaches welcome (please phone in advance).

BRYNKIR WOOLLEN MILL LTD.
Golan, Garndolbenmaen, Gwynedd, LL51 9YU. Tel: 01766 530236
Open: Easter – October; Monday – Friday, closed on bank holidays.
Ample free parking; buses and parties by prior arrangement.

The mill is set in the heart of the countryside between two of the prettiest valleys in Eryri (*Snowdonia*): Cwm Pennant and Chwm Ystradllyn. Water is taken from Afon Henwy to turn the water wheel and the 150 year old mill still produces a wide range of woollen goods.

The whole process can be viewed on the mill tour – the machines are operated in sequence by a local skilled workforce. There is also an opportunity to browse in the spacious shop with its large selection of Welsh woollens. The mill also has a shop to sell its goods on the Maes at Caernarfon.

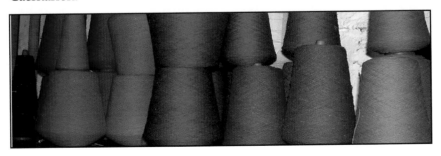

MELIN ESGAIR MOEL

Situated in the Museum of Welsh Life, St Fagans, Caerdydd (Cardiff), CF5 6XB.
Tel: 02920 573500   website: www.nmgw.ac.uk/mwl
Open 7 days a week, 10 a.m. – 5 p.m. throughout the year. Admission free.

An 18th century woollen mill relocated to the Museum of Welsh Life from Llanwrtyd, Powys. Machines are worked by craftsmen and include 18th century handlooms.

Products are for sale. Also on site: parking, cafe and all the attractions of the Museum of Welsh Life. Admission free.

CAMBRIAN WOOLLEN MILL AND VISITOR CENTRE

Llanwrtyd, Powys, LD5 4SD. Tel: 01591 610420 (Shop: 01591 610363)
website: www.cambrian-mill.co.uk
Open all year.

The mill lies beside Afon Irfon between the Cambrian Mountains and the Brecon Beacons. The factory was established in 1918 to give employment to ex-service men and women disabled in World War I. It offers a guided tour outlining the entire process – from shearing sheep and treating wool to weaving fabrics. Gift shop and restaurant. The Cambrian also produces the Welsh National tartan, St David's (*Brithwe Dewi Sant*) as well as the Welsh County and Family Name tartans.

MELIN DOLWERDD

Cwmpengraig, Dre-fach, nr Castellnewydd Emlyn (Newcastle Emlyn), *Sir Gaerfyrddin* (Carmarthenshire).
Tel: 01559 370874
Open: Monday – Saturday, 10 a.m. – 7 p.m.

A working woollen mill. Visitors can watch warping and weaving when in process. Guided tours can be arranged for adults by appointment. Admission free, mill shop, parking facilities.

ROCK MILLS
Capel Dewi, ger Llandysul, Dyffryn Teifi, SA44 4PH. Tel: 01559 362356

The old mill was built in 1890 by the great-grandfather of the present owner. The last of the Welsh mills to be powered by a water wheel. Tourist attraction and shop.

ELVET WOOLLEN MILL
Cynwyl Elfed, Sir Gaerfyrddin (Carmarthenshire). *Tel: 01267 281336*

A working woollen mill where warping, winding and weaving processes are undertaken. Guided tours can be arranged for groups only by appointment. Entrance fee.

MELIN GANOL
Solfach, Tyddewi (St Davids), Sir Benfro (Pembrokeshire), SA62 6XD. Tel: 01437 721112 e-mail: enquiries@solvawoollenmill.co.uk.

Established 1907 to produce floor rugs and carpets. Tourist attraction and shop. Open: Easter – September.

NEWTOWN TEXTILE MUSEUM

5-7 Commercial Street, Y Drenewydd (Newtown), *Powys, SY16 2BL.*
Tel: 01686 622024 (or Powys/and Museums: 01938 554656)
website: www.powysmuseums.powys.gov.uk
Open: May – September, 2 p.m. – 5 p.m.; parking nearby.
An old 19th century weaving shop now houses this museum, which also consists 6 weavers cottages. First opened in 1967, it was restored and extended in the 1990s to record the heritage of the industry in the town. Exhibitions and craft workshops.

ABBEY WOOLLEN MILL

Housed within the Swansea Maritime and Industrial Museum, Victoria Road, Abertawe (Swansea). *Tel: 01792 650351*
A fully operating mill producing woollen goods from raw fleece. Now closed but will be partly reopened at Y Felin Ddŵr, Parkmill, Gower.

CEREDIGION MUSEUM

Coliseum, Terrace Road, Aberystwyth, Ceredigion. Tel: 01970 633088
Permanent displays of carthenni, blankets and a traditional handloom. Admission free.
Open: Monday – Saturday, 10 a.m.-5 p.m.

MELIN PANT-YR-YNN

Bethania, Blaenau Ffestiniog, Gwynedd LL41 3LZ Tel: 01766 830540
This mill, with its huge 24' working water wheel is Blaenau Ffestiniog's earliest surviving slate mill. For the first twenty years of its life it was a slab mill for the Diffwys quarry. Then it became a school for seven years and later Jacob Jones' woollen mill until its closure in 1964. The building is virtually unchanged since then, but now includes an exhibition of watercolour drawings by Falcon D Hildred, recording the historic buildings, quarries and landscape of Blaenau Ffestiniog. Architectual antiques also on view. Open by arrangement. Admission £2.

AFON-WEN ANTIQUES AND CRAFT CENTRE

Afon-wen, nr Caerwys, Yr Wyddgrug (Mold), *CH7 5UB.*
Tel: 01352 720965
A large craft and antique shop housed in an old mill. Open 6 days a week, incl. bank holidays (closed Mondays); free parking; licensed restaurant.

MEIRION MILL SHOP

Dinas Mawddwy, Powys, SY20 9LS.   Tel: 01650 531311
Open all year: seven days a week, free admission.

An old woollen mill just outside the mountain village of Dinas Mawddwy in Meirionnydd now houses a well stocked shop and a café which serves home baked light meals throughout the day. The mill used water power from Afon Dyfi to produce woollen goods which were very important to the local economy. Traditionally woven quilts and rugs, tweed jackets, ties, hats, knitwear, sheepskin slippers and gloves now fill its shelves. Other goods and crafts represent the best of Welsh products and some decorative and useful accessories for the home and garden.

There is plenty of free parking at the site, also a children's playground.